TANK HUNTING AND DESTRUCTION

MILITARY TRAINING PAMPHLET
No. 42

Prepared under the direction of
The Chief of the Imperial General Staff

Published by

The Naval & Military Press Ltd

Unit 5 Riverside, Brambleside
Bellbrook Industrial Estate
Uckfield, East Sussex
TN22 1QQ England

Tel: +44 (0)1825 749494

www.naval-military-press.com
www.nmarchive.com

CONTENTS

(*Continued on page iii of cover*)

MILITARY TRAINING PAMPHLET No. 42.—1940.

TANK HUNTING AND DESTRUCTION

Object of pamphlet

This pamphlet is drafted as a guide and help to troops who have the determination and nerve to destroy tanks at close quarters.

1. Introduction

Tanks well served and boldly directed have established a superiority on the battlefield which is out of all proportion to their true value ; the problem is now to reduce this menace to its true perspective even when elaborate equipment is not available.

It has been proved that tanks, for all their hard skin, mobility and armament achieve their more spectacular results from their moral effect on half-hearted or ill-led troops. Consequently, troops which attempt to withstand tanks by adopting a purely passive role will fail in their task, or at the best only half complete it.

Tank hunting must be regarded as a sport—big game hunting at its best. A thrilling, albeit a dangerous sport, which if skilfully played is about as hazardous as shooting tiger on foot, and in which the same principles of stalk and ambush are followed.

2. Tank hunting and destruction

1. *German methods*

The German method of attack is generally to tap along the front with his reconnaissance troops until a weak spot is discovered. As soon as such a spot is located the crossing of the obstacle is effected and a small bridgehead is made. This bridgehead is subsequently widened and arrangements made for the passage of tanks, and more troops.

Subsequently, by using methods of infiltration and with a complete disregard for open flanks, the Germans attempt to push through their mobile troops, if necessary on a narrow front. These mobile troops consist of groups of from three to five tanks, often with anti-tank guns in support, preceded by motor cyclists as scouts and followed by a small party of lorried infantry. These mobile groups are sometimes assisted by their own reconnaissance and close support aircraft. The axis of advance of these parties will sooner or later be that of a well defined road. They make no attempt to clear or occupy the area in which they operate, but concentrate on quick and deep penetration to destroy communications and stores, disorganize headquarters, and generally to spread alarm through rumour. The number of enemy tanks operating in an area behind our own troops is nearly always exaggerated by rumour.

On meeting a block in a defile the Germans attempt to outflank the party defending the road block, by using the motor-cyclists, or by dismounting their lorry-carried infantry or the crews of the rear tanks.

By night these mobile columns cease their activities and go into " harbours," which are selected with a view to conceal-ment from the air ; such places as farms, woods and hamlets being chosen.

The possibility of tanks being landed from aircraft after a suitable aerodrome or landing ground has been captured by parachutists must also be considered.

3. Tanks and their characteristics

1. *Types*

German tanks are of many different types which vary in detail rather than principle. Typical examples are illustrated in Plates 1 and 2 (further details are given in Armoured Fighting Vehicles (British and Foreign) notified in A.C.Is. for week ending 21st February, 1940).

2. *Weaknesses*

The following remarks apply generally to tanks of all types, which in spite of their hard skin, mobility and armament have serious weaknesses. Among these are :—

    (a) *Blindness.* The only view available is through the driver's slit, the gunners' slits, and the commander's slit, all of which are small and the first at least fixed to the front. Their radius of vision is consequently limited. When the tank is closed down the crew have no observation at all immediately above the tank, or on the ground *within* a radius of approxi-mately 15 feet of the tank itself. If a tank is travel-ling with the lid open, small arms fire will soon make it close down. There is always the danger, however, that these blind spots will be covered by the fire of other tanks.

PLATE 1

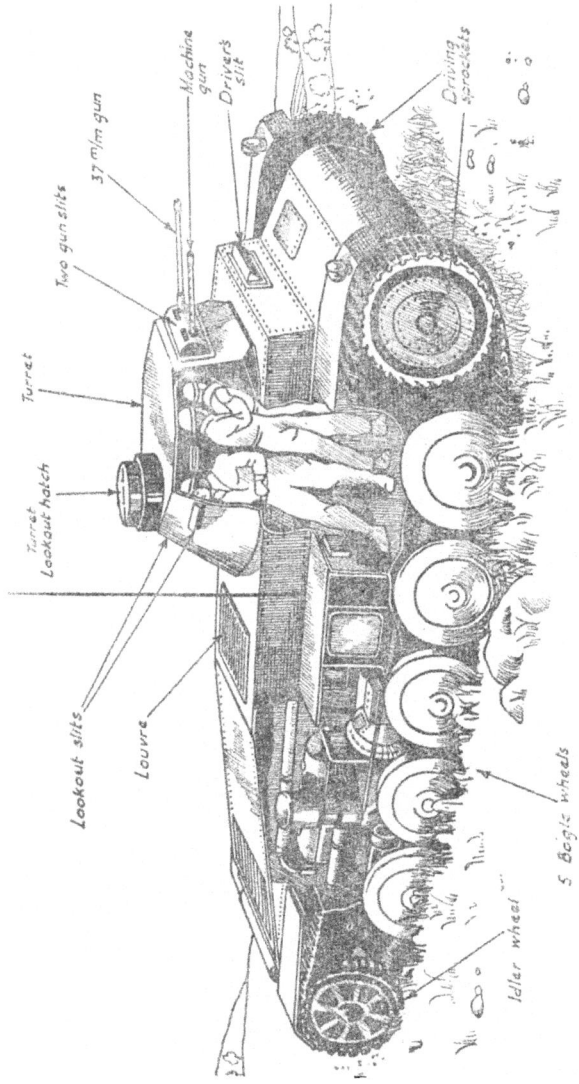

Turret
Turret Lookout hatch
Lookout slits
Louvre
5 Bogie wheels
Idler wheel
Two gun slits
37 m/m gun
Machine gun
Driver's slit
Driving sprockets

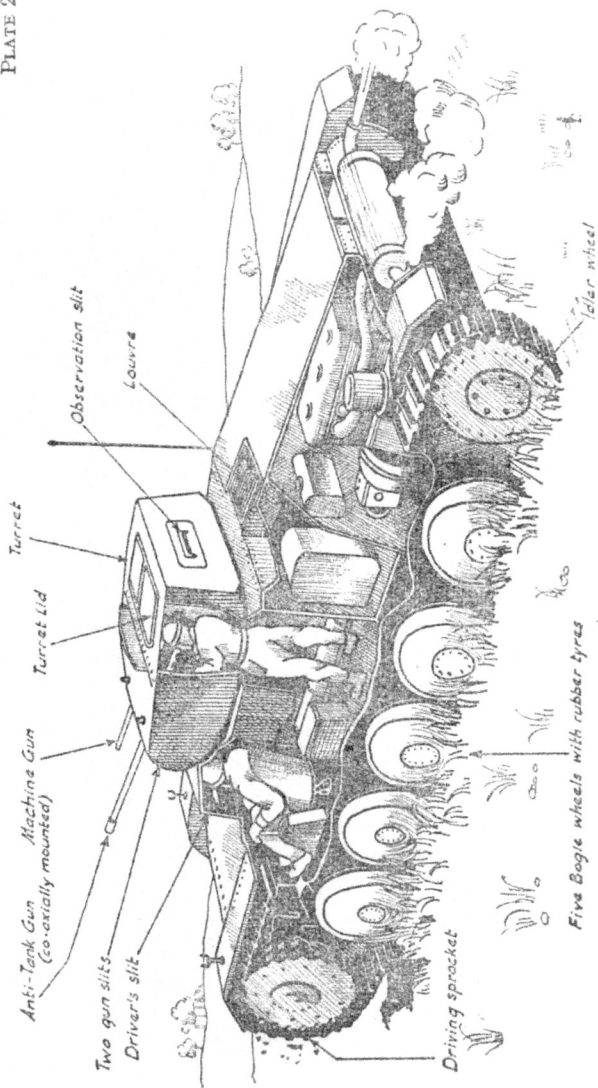

PLATE 2

4

Anti-Tank Gun   Machine Gun
(co-axially mounted)

Turret

Turret lid

Observation slit

Louvre

Two gun slits

Driver's slit

Driving sprocket

Idler wheel

Five Bogie wheels with rubber tyres

Note: In some cases a fixed gun is beside driver

(b) *Field of fire.* The guns are incapable of depression to fire on anything at ground level within an approximate radius of 20 feet of the vehicle or at elevation above 25 degrees. The tank cannot, therefore, engage targets in its immediate vicinity which are on the tops of high banks or in first floor windows of houses. The gun turrets revolve slowly and their weapons defend the vehicle from attack only along their immediate line of sight. A simultaneous attack, therefore, from several directions finds serious gaps in its defence. A tank is incapable of firing into deep slit trenches at any range, except in enfilade.

(c) *Tracks.* The vehicle is mobile only as long as its tracks hold out. If it is forced on to rough or stony ground by blocks or demolitions, wear increases rapidly; and the tracks of the heaviest tanks have been broken by direct hits from our anti-tank rifle. Percussion grenades containing approximately 3 lb. of explosive will break a track. Moreover, tracks may be removed by crowbars or wooden spars rammed in between the driving sprocket and the track whilst the vehicle is moving at a very slow pace. The British anti-tank mine will completely remove a track from any tank.

(d) *Crews.* The exhaustion of moving long distances and work for several hours in a closed tank is very considerable. The crews of tanks who have been in action require frequent rests for sleep and food; for which purpose they halt in concealment in harbours and lie about outside their vehicles.

(e) *Petrol.* The menace of a tank ceases when it runs out of petrol. Few tanks have a mileage of more than 100 miles without refilling. It is dependent for its supply on local petrol resources or on its own petrol lorries—which are unarmoured and easily set on fire by tracer ammunition or petrol bombs—or supply by air.

(f) *Night.* Darkness is the greatest ally of the tank hunter. This is the opportunity for stalking, sniping, and attacking with grenades and incendiary bombs. On no account must they be allowed to rest undisturbed. Movement by night is almost impossible unless the tank commander directs proceedings by sticking his head out through the open roof. If he does so he is vulnerable to any form of attack however primitive.

3. *Vulnerable points*

The following are as a rule the most vulnerable points in a tank :—

(a) *Driver's, gunners' and commander's slits*

At these points the tank is vulnerable to small arms fire and attack by flame throwers. In most tanks the openings are variable, and fire directed at them will cause the gap to be closed to a minimum, thus reducing visibility and ventilation.

These slits are often given some overhead protection to give additional cover against the usual trajectory of a bullet. For this reason small arms fire is most effective when directed from ground level at short range '' under the eyebrows.''

The slits are often protected with glasses which, though bullet-proof, must be replaced when hit. Reserve glasses carried are limited. Vision through the glasses is limited, and if they are used the slits are useless as a means of ventilation.

(b) *The belly and top of the tank*

The front and sides of a tank are as a rule the most heavily armoured parts ; the armour on the top is less heavy and that beneath the tank is thinnest of all. Opportunities may be presented for a shot by anti-tank rifle from ground level against this vulnerable part when a tank rears up to cross a bank or to climb from a ditch. Owing to the shape of the belly, fire must be at short range to ensure penetration.

(c) *The tracks*

See 2 para. (c), above.

(d) *The louvres or air vents*

These allow for the necessary intake of air for the engine and ventilation for the crew. If incendiary bombs are burst over these louvres, the provision of the necessary air is upset and the tank may be set on fire.

(e) *The turret*

Whenever possible the tank will drive with its turret open and the commander looking out. In this state it is very vulnerable to a surprise attack from above by incendiary bombs or ordinary grenades and other weapons, when passing through streets or under trees.

4. Tactical action against tanks

1. *General*

Before tanks can effect penetration of our defences it is likely that they will have to overcome a tank obstacle and that they will have been subjected to the fire of anti-tank guns and field artillery. In addition they may have suffered casualties from our anti-tank minefields. They may have been subjected to counter attack by our own tanks, which is the most effective answer to a tank attack.

Crews of enemy tanks which do subsequently succeed in breaking through must be harried, hunted, sniped and ambushed from the moment they are located until they are destroyed. They must be compelled to move with turrets closed and slits reduced to the minimum, which in itself will make it impossible for them to determine their position except in country which they know well.

Tank-hunting platoons will, however, as a rule be working on an area basis. They must exploit the advantages this gives them, and every platoon must have a thorough knowledge of the area in which it works. All tracks and by-paths must be known, suitable positions for ambushes and road blocks must be selected, and methods of attack on all likely tank harbours must be considered.

Although this task is primarily one for the specially equipped tank-hunting platoons, the responsibility is not theirs alone. Every soldier and every member of the Home Guard should be trained in the methods of tank hunting and in the use of special anti-tank weapons. The lessons of Spain and Finland confirm that tanks can be destroyed by men who have the bravery, resource and determination to do so.

Tank-hunting platoons must retain their mobility and make use of it to act offensively against enemy tanks. They should not be used for the defence of road blocks with a prepared tank obstacle if other troops can be made available for the purpose.

2. *Anti-tank weapons*

Apart from anti-tank guns and artillery there are many other weapons for use against tanks and in connection with tank hunting which should be understood by all :—

(a) *Anti-tank rifle* (*see* S.A.T. Vol. 1, Pamphlet No. 5)

The anti-tank rifle penetrates the armour of the light tank, and that of some heavier models when fired at short range. It is effective against the tracks of the heaviest tanks yet encountered.

(b) *Small arms fire*

Small arms fire is effective against the commander's, driver's and gunners' slits. It is most effective when fired from ground level at short range " under the eyebrows."

(c) *Molotov bombs*

These are hand-made bombs consisting of a bottle containing various inflammable mixtures of petrol, tar and other substances and a means for igniting the mixture when the bottle is smashed. (Details are given in Appendix A.) These bombs should be directed above the louvres or vents so that the burning liquid may be sucked into the tank to make it uninhabitable or possibly to set the vehicle on fire. It is important to aim high at the tank so that the liquid can flow downwards. The first inclination to throw the bomb hard at the tank must be avoided ; an underarm lob will often be the best method of throwing unless the bomb can be dropped from the windows of a house or some other position above the tank. After the first bomb has hit the target and ignited, successive bombs can be thrown without themselves being ignited.

(d) *The phosphorus grenade* ("The A.W. Grenade ")

This is an improved type of " Molotov bomb," which ignites spontaneously as soon as the glass is shattered, producing an incendiary mixture and a dense cloud of smoke. (Details are given in Appendix B). The grenade may be used as follows :—

i. It may be thrown at tanks, vehicles, buildings, pillboxes, etc., in order to blind the occupants with smoke and possibly expel them. The grenade should be thrown at the front of the tank; the mixture remaining on the tank continues to burn and give off smoke from which the tank cannot escape by movement.

ii. In favourable wind conditions a controlled smoke screen can be put up near a road block or pillbox by placing the grenades in suitable positions and exploding them by small arms fire.

iii. The grenade has considerable incendiary effect owing to its phosphorus content, which can only be completely destroyed by allowing it to burn itself out. It can be temporarily extinguished with water, but will start burning again after it has dried, on being disturbed.

(e) *The sticky (S.T.) grenade.* This is a high explosive grenade with a five-second time fuze. It is designed to stick on impact and to shatter the armour or track on explosion. (Details are given in Appendix C.) The safest and easiest way of using these grenades is by dropping them from an upstairs window ; they may also be used from an ambush or trench within 10 to 15 yards of a tank. A position on a bank controlling a road has obvious advantages. When it is possible to close with the tank under cover of smoke or darkness the grenade may be placed by hand as described in Appendix C.

(f) *The anti-tank percussion grenade.* The hand percussion grenade is a simple H.E.grenade with an instantaneous percussion fuze. It consists of about 3 lb. of explosive, and, being in a light casing only, there is no shrapnel effect, the danger to the thrower being mainly from the blast. (Details of the grenade are given in Appendix D.) The grenades should be thrown whenever possible into the tracks of the tank, alternative targets being the wheels at either end of the track, the plating over the engine or any of the observation slits.

Grenades should be thrown into the tracks as far forward as possible, as in the case of a forward break the tank will quickly run off its track and must be jacked up before the track can be replaced.

(g) *Harvey flame thrower.* This flame thrower consists of a vertical cylinder of 22 gallons capacity mounted on wheels in the same manner as a porter's barrow. To the cylinder is connected 25 feet of flexible hose terminating in a nozzle ; a rest is provided on which the pipe carrying the nozzle can be traversed and elevated. (For detailed description *see* Appendix E). When in operation, a jet of inflammable liquid, which is ignited on leaving the nozzle, is thrown to a range of approximately 50 yards ; the maximum' range gradually decreases as the cylinder is expended.

These flame throwers will be of value mainly as part of the defensive equipment of fixed road blocks and will generally be best sited when placed on the flank on the enemy side of the road block. They will be of particular value in dealing with tanks beyond the range of the A.W. grenade and Molotov bombs.

It may be possible on occasion to mount the equipment in a car or truck for mobile use.

(*h*) *The Northover (bottle) mortar.* This is a simple mortar designed to throw the A.W. grenade to ranges of between 50 and 150 yards. (Details are given in Appendix F.) It will be of use for attacking tanks, when it is impossible to get to close quarters. It should not be used prematurely to give away an ambush or to disclose the position of a road block.

(*i*) *Anti-tank mines.* All men should understand the mechanism and use of the various anti-tank mines which may be available. (*See* Military Training Pamphlet No. 40.) Anti-tank mines (Mk. II or IV) may be joined together by means of wire or rope and nets to form a string of mines which can be drawn across a road at short notice.

3. *Getting to close quarters*

The destruction and immobilization of tanks by grenades and bombs demands ability by the attacker to get at close quarters to the tank. He can do this in various ways :—

(*a*) *From trenches*

During an enemy tank attack over trenches, the enemy tanks will often be within a few yards of men who can immobilize them ;

(*b*) *From ambushes*

Tanks passing through villages and other defiles will often place themselves within range ;

(*c*) *By the use of smoke*

Smoke may be used to blind tanks and under its cover a determined man may get at close quarters across the open ;

(*d*) *By fieldcraft*

A tank cannot fire in all directions at the same time. (A tank with turret guns only is limited to firing in one direction. If, in addition, it has a fixed gun beside the driver, it is also capable of fire direct to its front.) If men work together approaching the tank from different angles, moving only when the guns are not directed at them and at other times making use of cover, they should always be able to close with a single tank which is stationary or moving slowly. To do so they must watch carefully the movements of the tank's guns and carefully select beforehand their bounds from cover to cover.

4. *Destruction of tanks at close quarters*

Having got close to the tank it may be attacked with incendiary and H.E. bombs—or a steel rail may be pushed in between the track and the driving sprocket with the object of stripping the track. The tank being now immobilized, the crew must be killed or captured. Incendiary bombs burst over the louvres may force them into the open, as also may anti-tank percussion grenades. If this does not hurry out the crew, a " S.T. " grenade may be exploded on the roof of the tank, and a No. 36 or other grenade dropped through the hole made. Failing this, rifles may be fired into the slits at point blank range.

5. *Attacks on tanks in harbours*

As night approaches the small enemy columns will seek suitable harbours for the night. These will be selected with a view to concealment from both ground and air and for economy of men in protective duties. Farms, woods and hamlets are likely places. The defence of harbours will vary according to the men and tanks available, the ground, fatigue of the crews and other factors. The tanks may be protected by a thin outpost line of dismounted troops, although even then the tanks will be sited tactically and their guns manned ; in other cases the tanks may be used to provide the outposts, being sited to cover all approaches. At other times when very fatigued they may rely almost entirely on concealment, with little protection except one or two sentries close to the tanks.

Tank hunters should attempt to get into positions from which they can note in detail the enemy's dispositions and plan their night attack. This reconnaissance is of the greatest importance. In carrying out this attack their primary objective will be the men as the tanks are unlikely to be fully manned, and even if manned will be of little fighting value in the darkness. Once the men are killed or captured, the destruction of the tanks should be easy. The method of attack will be similar to that carried out by other fighting patrols, except that weapons for tank destruction will be carried. This should not be regarded as a specialist task to be carried out only by tank hunting platoons, but as one which may be carried out by any troops. Should enemy columns try to harbour and rest by day and be too strong for a direct attack, they must be harassed remorselessly by

snipers, mortars, bombing from the air, and all other means
available so that rest is impossible for them. In the mean-
time, plans to ambush them when they do move should be
made.

6. *Rendering a captured tank unserviceable*

A tank crew may be put out of action or captured, leaving
the tank itself intact. When possible, captured tanks should
be salvaged for examination by experts, but if there is any
possibility of the tank again falling into enemy hands it
should be rendered unserviceable. This may be done in a
number of ways, including the following :—

  (a) By fire—flame-producing bombs being dropped inside
       the tank—will often be the quickest method, but
       not always the most desirable.

  (b) Breaking or removing the tracks is effective for a
       short period and until spare parts are available.

  (c) To put the tank out of action for a prolonged period
       the following methods are recommended :—

       i. breaking water jacket of engine with sledge
          hammer ;

       ii. smashing the driver's controls, including the
           gear lever ;

       iii. smashing the carburettor or fuel pump ;

       iv. throwing H.E. bombs inside the tank ;

       v. if it is impossible to open the tank one of the
          sprockets may be blown off with gelignite.

7. *Keeping touch*

It will not always be possible for tank hunters to attack
an enemy column. If they cannot do so the enemy must be
shadowed and stalked and information must be passed to
other troops in the area with regard to the enemy strength
(which must not be exaggerated), the direction in which he
is moving, his method of advance and other points which
will aid others to destroy them. Early information with
regard to the movement of enemy columns is important to
enable tank hunters to prepare their ambushes. Tank-hunting
platoon commanders must work in the closest co-operation
with the battalion intelligence section not only to get the
information they require but also to pass on information
gained by them to others. A system of light signals may
also be developed for passing information and arrangements
made for intercommunication between tank hunters and
aircraft.

5. Road blocks, ambushes and obstacles

1. *Road blocks*

(a) *General*

  i. Roads can be blocked against WHEELED vehicles in various ways :—

    (a) By cratering.

    (b) By a barricade of local materials such as farm carts, harrows, etc., or by debris from demolished buildings.

    (c) By felling trees. Trees felled to form road blocks should be left with the trunks attached to the stumps, if possible. To effect this, no cut should be made on the side to which the tree is to fall, and, unless the tree will fall naturally in the required direction, it must be strained with guys.

    (d) By coils of concertina wire opened out and bent into U shape to fill the breadth of the road.

    (e) By trenches across the road.

  ii. To stop TANKS a more formidable obstacle will be necessary. 80 lb. of explosive at a depth of 6 ft. in average ground makes a crater 7 ft. deep and at least 20 ft. wide. This size of crater is likely to be an effective obstacle. No normal tree or series of trees felled across a road can be relied on to stop a tank, nor can any rapidly erected wireblock. Light road blocks may, however, be made effective against tanks by the inclusion of anti-tank mines.

  iii. The effectiveness of all blocks depends on their being located in defiles and kept under constant observation and fire. They should also, whenever possible, be sited to achieve surprise.

(b) *Siting*

    Sites should be selected in which it is difficult for crews of approaching vehicles to see the obstacle until they are close to it, or to turn round or move off the road once they have seen it. For example, defiles where the road passes between woods, deep ditches, thick hedges, high banks or buildings are suitable, particularly if there is a bend in the road close to the enemy side of the obstacle.

    It is an advantage if the points at which tanks are

14

PLATE 3

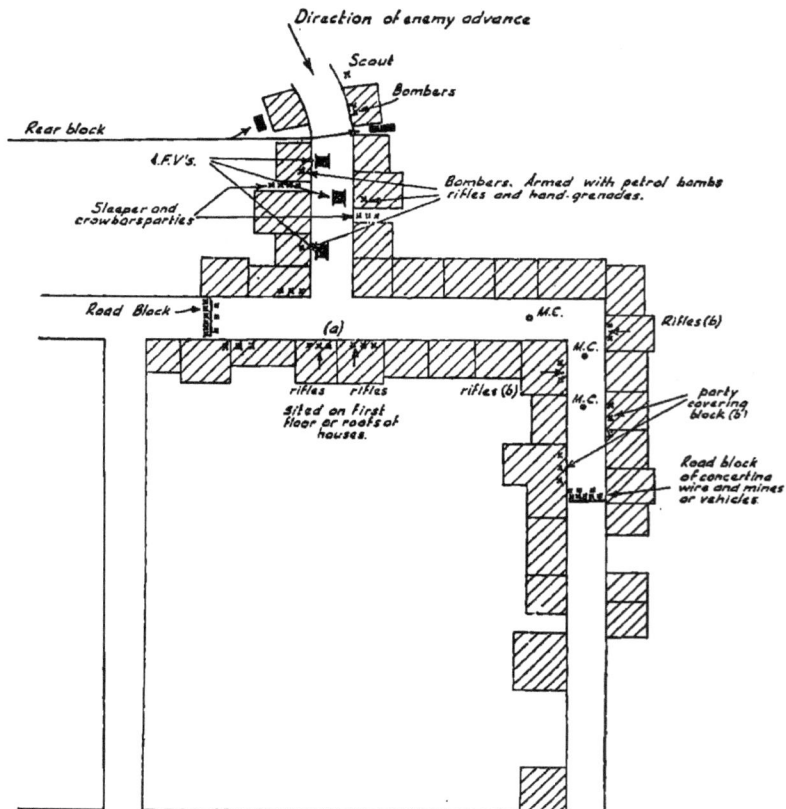

Diagrammatic Layout of ambush in village

Direction of enemy advance

Scout

Bombers

Rear block

A.F.V's.

Bombers. Armed with petrol bombs rifles and hand-grenades.

Sleeper and crowbars parties

Road Block

(a)

M.C.

Rifles (b)

M.C.

rifles   rifles   rifles (b)

M.C.

party covering block (b)

Sited on first floor or roofs of houses.

Road block of concertina wire and mines or vehicles.

NOTE: The party at (a) should not disclose their position till after the leading M.C's. or lighter armoured cars have been stopped by the Road Block.   These will then be engaged by the parties at (b).   This will prevent the warning being passed back by the M.C's. before the A.F.V's. have walked into the trap.
    The rear block may consist of lorries laden with stone which can be put into low gear and crashed across the road.

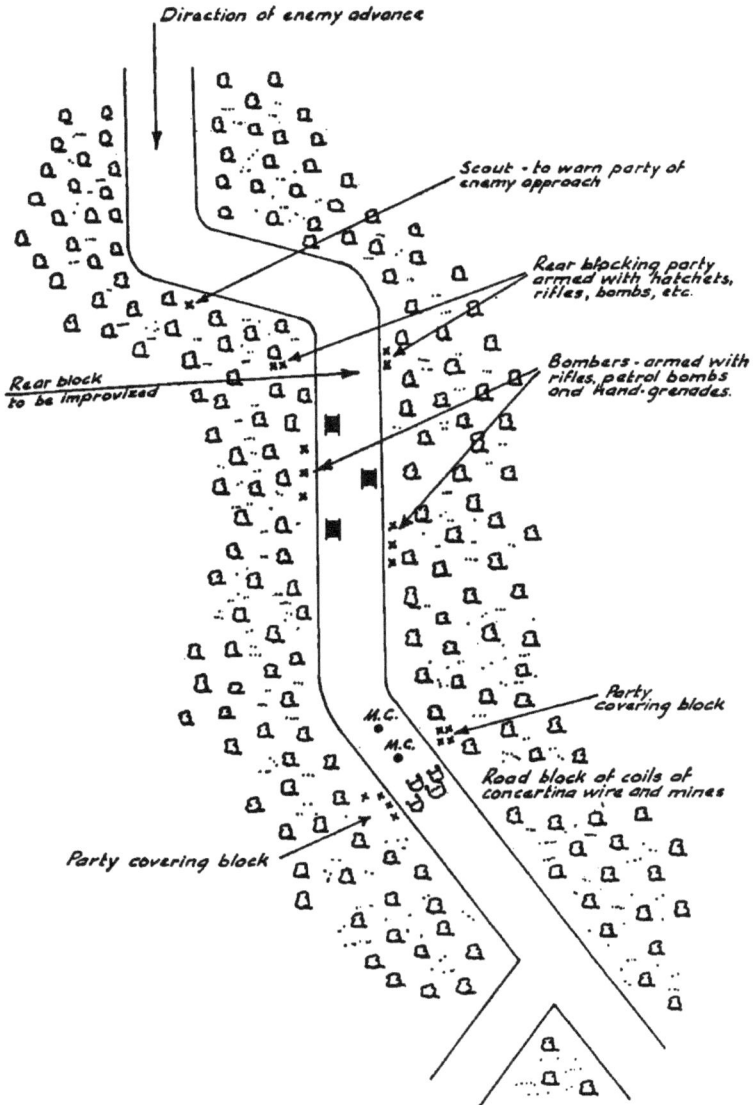

Diagrammatic Layout of ambush in wood.

PLATE 4

Direction of enemy advance

Scout - to warn party of enemy approach

Rear blocking party armed with hatchets, rifles, bombs, etc.

Rear block to be improvized

Bombers - armed with rifles, petrol bombs and hand-grenades.

M.C.

M.C.

Party covering block

Road block of coils of concertina wire and mines

Party covering block

likely to stop are overlooked at close range so that
the tanks can be bombed from above, or if there are
gaps between buildings or other cover at these points
from which bombs can be thrown or rails pushed into
the tracks.

The sides of the defile should be closed by natural
obstacles or barbed wire to keep enemy dismounted
personnel in full view of the defenders and to prevent
them from breaking out at the side and stalking the
garrison.

Occasionally, if the road passes through long
defiles, it may be possible to set traps by placing
the obstacle well inside the defile and preparing a
block at its entrance which can be rapidly put into
position after the enemy vehicle has passed.

Pillboxes and ground floor windows straight behind
an obstacle should be avoided, though they may be
used as bait in the form of dummy positions. These
are likely to be in full view of the crew with the
weapons of the A.F.V. pointing at them. The best
positions to occupy will usually be in upper windows,
or on roofs or behind banks on the flanks of the
obstacle. Pillboxes should be well camouflaged and
sited to cover the obstacle. The position chosen
will depend on the ground and may be to the flank
of the obstacle; behind it if well concealed, or even
on the enemy side. The upper windows of houses
and the bank on the flanks of the obstacle should also
be occupied.

(c) *Defence of the block*

Like all obstacles, road blocks must be covered with
fire. One section, with, if possible, an anti-tank rifle,
will often be a sufficient garrison. Anti-tank rifles,
L.M.Gs. and tommy guns should be sited away from
the block and on the flanks covering the road on the
enemy side; tank bombers should be in position
on the flanks of the defile on the enemy side of the
block. Snipers should be disposed to attack any
enemy leaving his A.F.V.; remaining personnel
should be distributed to prevent any outflanking
movement by the enemy. Consideration must be
given to the possibility of smoke being used by
enemy tanks to conceal their movements, and
weapons sited accordingly.

Although hostile A.F.Vs. may be expected from
a certain direction, it is always possible they may

17

appear where least expected. Consideration should
therefore be given to alternative positions to meet
possible situations.

Where no natural cover from fire exists, garrisons
of road blocks should dig weapon pits for their own
protection.

2. *Ambushes*

In every area, suitable sites for ambushes both for the
A.F.Vs. and their accompanying personnel should be recon
noitred, planned in detail and, where desirable, the necessary
material placed ready at the site. Suitable points for
ambushes will generally be found in defiles such as villages,
towns, cuttings and woods.

The essence of a good ambush is surprise ; it cannot
therefore be made a subject for rules. If ambushes are
prepared by fixed drill methods they will cease to be ambushes.
They must therefore be devised by the ingenuity of individual
leaders who must pit their wits against those of the enemy.
The object must always be to mystify and mislead—obvious
places should be avoided.

Time for preparation will often be short and tank-hunting
platoons must therefore be able to prepare an ambush with
the minimum of equipment, and often with their weapons
alone.

The variations of an ambush are almost unlimited. For
example, sometimes it will be advisable to attack reconnoitring motor cyclists ; at other times the ambushers may
hide until the enemy motor cyclists have passed through and
then attack the tanks, while at other times the whole column
may be allowed to pass and may then be attacked from the
rear. Sometimes it may be possible to draw the enemy from
his line of advance into a trap.

An ambush in its simplest form may consist of a few men
concealed at intervals along the side of the road. At a given
signal they throw their A.W. bombs to blind the tanks
and then attack with hand percussion bombs. Somebody
should be ready to deal with the enemy motor cyclists as
they come racing back to see what has happened.

The basis of the plan will often be :—

(a) To surprise and overcome the reconnoitring motor
cyclists before they are able to warn the leading tank.
A wire stretched taut across the road 3 feet from the
ground will often be sufficient. If possible, these
motor cyclists should be disposed of silently, and
devices for puncturing their tyres will sometimes be

useful (e.g., boards with upturned nails, broken glass, etc.) ;

(b) To attack tanks individually and to prevent them supporting each other. Bends in the roads may make this possible ; if not, one alternative is to make use of smoke bombs to isolate individual tanks. Having isolated a tank it may be attacked with incendiary bombs and high explosive grenades until it is destroyed. In village streets, woods and other narrow defiles speed of action, surprise and a simultaneous attack on supporting tanks may render the isolation of individual tanks unnecessary ;

(c) The provision of " look outs " to protect the ambushing detachments from lorried infantry following the tanks. The action of the enemy infantry when the leading tanks have met an ambush is likely to be to deploy with the intention of taking the ambushers in flank or rear.

(d) Arrangements for the withdrawal of the party and getting them once more under control so that they may prepare fresh ambushes and continue the fight. These arrangements will include the selection of a rendezvous (which should be known to every man), the parking of vehicles, bicycles, etc., with a view to the " get-away " and signals for withdrawal.

3. *Petrol ambushes*

Petrol and oil poured on to a road and ignited will, in suitable conditions, form an effective ambush, the intense heat and flame resulting in the destruction or immobilization of enemy vehicles.

The use of this means is restricted to defiles which the enemy are likely to use (e.g., to debouch from the coast or landing grounds). Consideration must be given to the effect of fires which may be started in the vicinity.

The method of employment is by gravity or trailer pump from a reservoir hidden and protected at a distance from but within view of the defile. Surprise is important and the reservoir should be camouflaged. The oil is led by 2-inch pipes to the defile, discharged from jets or sprays and ignited electrically or by some other simple means. The composition recommended is 25 per cent. petrol and 75 per cent. gas oil, which being of no value for the propulsion of motor vehicles is of little use to the enemy.

The reservoirs may be static or mobile, preferably the latter —any tank with the necessary capacity may be used either mounted on a lorry or built into a previously prepared position. Fuel is required on a scale of 2 gallons per square foot per hour. Thus to cover an area of road 50 feet long by 20 feet wide requires 200 gallons for every 6 minutes burning. To sustain a fire of great intensity a head of oil of only a few feet is necessary and a pump is not an essential.

This form of ambush should be prepared only where approved by general officers commanding-in-chief or such officers to whom they may delegate the authority.

4. *Bluffs and booby traps*

Every possible device must be used to slow up the movement of enemy mobile columns and to stop tanks and make them disembark part of their crews who can then be shot. Motor cyclists, though often a difficult target to hit when on the move, are very vulnerable when halted. The defence has achieved much if it can make the task of the reconnoitring motor cyclist so dangerous that the tanks themselves must lead the column. The intention should be to instil into the enemy such a fear of ambushes that he will approach every defile and bend in a road with caution, and that he will make a dismounted reconnaissance before attempting to pass such points, which are abundant in the close country of Britain. Once this moral ascendancy has been achieved the danger of tank infiltration is over.

The following are examples of bluffs and booby traps which must, of course, be combined with road ambushes :—

(a) Dummy anti-tank mines—the surface of a road broken up as though the road had been mined or even a row of upturned soup plates will demand dismounted reconnaissance. The enemy making the reconnaissance may be sniped ;

(b) a number of blankets slung across a village street, which might be concealing a road block or ambush, will probably stop a tank at least once ;

(c) dummy pillboxes will be of value to draw both the enemy's attention and his fire and so to give the tank hunters an opportunity to get to close quarters with their bombs ;

(d) strips of canvas may be laid across a road to conceal a trench, or to explode bombs when moved. They may prove equally effective if they are no more than harmless strips of canvas. Hay or straw spread over a stretch of road may be used in a similar way.

(e) Booby traps consisting of road mines, charges for felling trees, or bombs designed to burst in the foliage of trees above tanks and exploded by a trip wire across the road, are described in Field Engineering Pamphlet No. 6.

Whenever booby traps are prepared, the danger to our own troops must always be considered, and adequate precautions must be taken to prevent them falling into the traps set for the enemy.

5. *Tank obstacles*

(a) *Anti-tank mines*

Anti-tank mines play the same part against A.F.Vs. as wire does against infantry. The principles of its employment are similar. Unless covered by the fire of the defenders, anti-tank mines are in most cases useless. In road blocks in particular the efficiency of the obstacle will depend largely on the skill with which the covering weapons are sited.

Tanks on discovering a mined road block will usually try to work round it, drive off the defending troops and then remove the mines. To counter this the mines should be placed so that they are encountered unexpectedly and where deviation is awkward. Close spacing should be used.

(b) *Other tank obstacles*

The size of the obstacle required to stop a tank depends on the design and dimensions of the tank concerned. The following are the guiding rules :—

 i. A tank cannot cross a gap which is appreciably wider than half the overall length of the tank ; unless it can approach at speed, when it may be able to jump an appreciable distance.

 ii. A tank cannot climb a solid vertical face which is higher than the top of the tank's track where it passes over the leading sprocket or idler wheel ; in the case of trenches and earth banks the height of the vertical face should be not less than 5 feet.

 iii. A tank is unlikely to surmount an obstacle which causes the ground line of the tank to be tilted, from the forward end, to an angle of 45 degrees with the horizontal. This rule governs the ability of a tank to surmount an obstacle placed on a slope.

(c) *Trees*

Single rows of trees to withstand the thrust of a
medium tank should consist of trees of not less
than 18 inches in diameter. In the case of a copse
where a series of trees in depth exists the effective
diameter of trees can be reduced to 8 inches. Modern
tanks can manœuvre in very restricted space and
can pass through gaps of from 6 ft. to 8 ft.

Trees of the diameter required, whether in single
rows or copses, will seldom be found growing at
close enough intervals to prevent tanks manœuvring
between them. Artificial obstacles will, therefore,
usually be necessary to reduce the gaps, to close
rides, etc. The anti-tank mine is the simplest weapon
for this purpose.

(d) *Stumps*

Tree stumps will stop tanks when they are sturdy
enough to raise the tracks off the ground by fouling
the belly of the tank between the tracks. For this
purpose, stumps should be not less than 12 inches
in diameter and should be 2 ft. 3 ins. in height.
To prevent tanks manœuvring between stumps
the gaps must be reduced as in the case of trees.
Belts of stumps must possess some depth ; a single
line will not stop tanks.

(e) *Natural obstacles*

These include rivers, banks, woods and the
cuttings and embankments of railways and roads,
which if not in themselves of adequate dimensions
may often be made so with little labour.

(f) *Artificial obstacles*

Details of the construction of artificial obstacles
will be found in Military Training Pamphlet No. 43.

6. Training

Training must aim at producing quick-witted, bold, confident
and swift-moving teams of high morale. The following should
be included in the syllabus :—

(a) *Physical training*. Physical fitness of the highest
order is essential. Every man must be " fighting fit."

(b) *Fieldcraft*. Success will depend largely on fieldcraft.
The training described in Military Training Pamphlet
No. 33 should be carried out and applied to the special
task in view. For example, all men should be

practised in stalking a tank, individually and working in pairs. A "mock up" turret should be made which can be carried on a car or carrier. The men should then be taught to watch the tank's guns and to run forward from cover to cover whenever the guns are aiming in another direction. Similar exercises should be carried out against a pair of tanks, making use of smoke.

(c) *Night work.* During darkness the A.F.V. loses almost all the advantages it may have by day over the man on his feet. Tank-hunting platoons should specialize in night work (*see* Military Training Pamphlet No. 33). Exercises should include attacks on tanks, whether halted, on the move or in harbour, and sections should be pitted against each other, acting as enemy in turns.

(d) *Map reading.* A high standard is essential.

(e) *Ambush training.* The art of siting, preparing and manning ambushes in villages, woods and other types of country should be practised. There must, however, be no stereotyped plan. The success of an ambush depends on surprise and depends on wits rather than rules.

(f) *Field engineering.* Men should be trained in the field engineering required in the construction of road blocks, e.g., use of concertina wire, the felling of trees, tank traps, etc. A general knowledge of the use of explosives should be included.

(g) *Recognition of A.F.Vs.* It is essential that men should be able to recognize allied and enemy A.F.Vs. and their types. (*See* Pamphlet notified in A.C.Is. for week ending 21st February, 1940.) They should know the weak spots in enemy tanks.

(h) *Weapon training.* All members of tank hunting detachments should be trained in the use of the special anti-tank weapons with which they are armed, in addition to the L.M.G., rifle, bayonet, grenade, 2-inch mortar and anti-tank rifle. A good proportion of expert snipers should be included, and the use of smoke should be practised. Dummy bombs of approximately the correct weight should be made up locally of sand, etc., sacking containers, and men practised in throwing them at the tracks of carriers.

(j) *Anti-tank mines.* (*See* Military Training Pamphlet No. 40.)

THE ANTI-TANK PETROL BOMB
" MOLOTOV COCKTAIL "

The bomb consists of a glass bottle containing a mixture of petrol and other inflammable substances, and a means of ignition.

i. *Ingredients*

In its simplest form the inflammable substance consists of petrol and tar in approximately equal proportions, but this may be varied by the addition of naphtha, paraffin, Diesel oil, etc., which will make the substance cling more to the surface of the tank. The essentials are that it should be sufficiently volatile to ignite easily while having sufficient body so that the duration of burning will be adequate. Duration of burning may be increased by the inclusion of a small proportion of sawdust, cotton waste, etc.

ii. *Bottles*

Any bottle which will break easily of approximately 1 pint size will do (e.g. whisky, sherry, lime juice bottles) ; the 1 pint beer bottle being more difficult to break is less suitable. Large bottles such as quart beer bottles and champagne bottles are difficult both to throw and to break. Bottles should be given two or three scratches with a diamond down their length to make them break more easily. Circular scratches should not be made.

iii. *Ignition*

There are various methods of ignition : the materials used to be satisfactory must satisfy the conditions that they can be ignited in a wind, will not go out when the bottle is thrown or broken, and will not be affected by damp, etc. The following are examples which have proved satisfactory :—

(a) *Lifeboat matches*

Two Lifeboat matches bound to the bottle with adhesive tape. Matches liable to be affected by damp may be covered by cellophane paper held in position by rubber bands. The fuzees are lighted with an ordinary matchbox and must be burning well rather than fuzing before the bomb is thrown.

(b) *Cinema film*

     A length of about 18 inches of cinema film allowed to curl round the bottle and fixed at one end with adhesive tape may be used. Ignition can be by match or cigarette end, but again it must be burning well before the bomb is thrown.

(c) *Cotton waste or rag*

     Cotton waste or rag tied to the bottle may be used. This should be soaked previously in paraffin and immediately before use dipped in petrol or the inflammable mixture from the bomb.

THE SELF-IGNITING PHOSPHORUS GRENADE

THE A.W. GRENADE

1. *Characteristics*

The self-igniting phosphorus grenade is an improved type of " Molotov cocktail." It is hand thrown and weighs 1½ lb. On striking a hard object, the glass container breaks and the contents ignite giving forth clouds of smoke and considerable heat ; unless the glass is broken, the grenade will not ignite.

2. Description

The grenade consists of a short-necked half-pint clear glass bottle containing yellow phosphorus, benzene, rubber and water with a free space of 10 per cent. It is sealed with a plain red crown cork.

The grenade ignites spontaneously as soon as the glass is shattered owing to the oxidation of the phosphorus in air which causes sufficient heat to ignite the benzene.

A 2-inch strip of crude rubber gradually dissolves in the container during storage and makes the contents tacky ; this assists the liquid to adhere to the object at which the grenade is directed.

3. *Packing*

24 grenades are packed in one wire-bound wooden partitioned case measuring 21·5 in. by 13 75 in. by 9·25 in.

Gross weight of case filled, 53 lb.

The case has two rope handles and is fastened with two wires sealed with lead seals.

The fastening can quickly be broken with a jack-knife, or similar instrument.

The top of the box is stencilled or branded :—

HANDLE WITH CARE

A.W. BOMBS.

FRAGILE GLASS.

DO NOT DROP.

HIGHLY INFLAMMABLE.

An enamelled metal plate is screwed to the inside of the lid giving full instructions of storage and fire precautions.

4. *Action*

When the glass is shattered an instantaneous ignition takes place, a dense cloud of choking fumes (phosphorus pentoxide and sulphur dioxide) is liberated. The grenade should therefore be thrown so that the wind does not blow the fumes back and obscure the vision of the thrower.

The grenade can be thrown like a hand grenade, but it must be remembered that it needs sharp contact with a hard surface to shatter the glass so as to ignite the contents.

Thrown against a tank the glass will break and the grenade ignite, but thrown along a tarmac road the grenade rolls on to a standstill and does not break ; therefore it does not ignite and could easily be thrown back.

5. *Storage and transport*

Whenever possible, cases should be stored under water, e.g., streams, ditches, ponds or, where this is not possible, in a cool place. In no circumstances must they be stored in houses. In any event a water supply must be readily available in case of accident. Grenades should be examined at frequent intervals and should any cracked glass appear, the grenade concerned should be destroyed forthwith. Fires can be extinguished with chemical extinguishers or water.

Great care must be exercised in handling these grenades whether in storage or in transit and in no circumstance should the crown cork be removed from the top of the bottle.

Grenades should be transported in open lorries and NOT by rail.

6. *Method of treating phosphorus burns*

(1) Wash with dilute alkali solution such as ordinary washing soda to neutralize phosphoric acid.

(2) Wash with 1 per cent. solution of copper sulphate and remove the resulting dark-coloured copper phosphide with forceps.

(3) Wash with antiseptic solution—boric acid or phenodine.

(4) Irradiate with ultra-violet light, if available.

(5) Apply picric acid dressings as for burns generally.

The detailed description of the method is as follows :

Wash the burn immediately with a solution of sodium carbonate, 2 tablespoonfuls to a pint of water. The treatment neutralizes any phosphoric acid formed as a result of the combustion of the phosphorus, and partially destroys any free phosphorus present. To free the burn from all traces of phosphorus, wash with 1 per cent. solution of copper sulphate. Copper sulphate combines with any free phosphorus, forming copper phosphide, thus preventing further ignition. Remove the resulting dark-coloured deposit with the aid of forceps and thoroughly wash with water containing a little antiseptic, boric acid or phenodine.

For extensive burns the use of ultra-violet radiation is very effective. If an ultra-violet lamp is available, dry the affected part and give 1 to 1½ minutes exposure to the light at about 2 feet away. Then apply strips of lint soaked in picric acid solution each day for 3 or 4 days and continue dressing with boric ointment as for ordinary burns. Before each redressing wash with boric acid lotion or phenodine in tepid water until the wound is quite clean. Phosphorus burns suppurate much more than ordinary burns.

For healing, period is usually about three to four weeks.

THE S.T. GRENADE

General description. The S.T. grenade is a form of hand grenade intended primarily for use against A.F.Vs. It is so designed as to stick to a suitable target thus ensuring that the high explosive with which it is filled has the maximum effect.

Weighing 2¼ lb. without its cover, the grenade itself consists of a spherical container 4 inches in diameter with handle attached. The spherical container, which is a glass flask encased in a sticky envelope, holds about 1½ lb. of a specially prepared nitro-glycerine explosive having a consistency about equal to that of vaseline.

Fitted inside the neck of the flask is an aluminium cup containing the detonator assembly. This assembly includes a percussion cap, 5-second fuze, detonator, and C.E. pellet.

The moulded throwing handle, which is attached to the outside of the neck of the flask by means of a screwed ring, contains a striker with a " Mills " type of release. This " Mills " handle fits snugly against the side of the throwing handle and is kept in position by a safety pin which affords additional protection by interfering with the movement of the striker head when it is in position. The safety pin has a label attached stating " Danger. Do not remove this pin until the grenade is to be thrown."

To protect the grenade until it is required for use it is fitted with an outer metal casing which completely encloses the spherical container, consisting of two hemispheres hinged at the bottom. This casing springs apart and drops off when the pin or clip is withdrawn.

For protection in transit the joint in the casing may in the earlier models be covered with adhesive tape, which is carried round the neck of the casing. This tape must, of course, be removed before the casing can be released.

Method of issue. S.T. grenades are packed in metal cases, each case containing five grenades. The end of each case is lettered " 5 S.T. grenades," with an indication that the grenades are filled. Other indications referring to various stages of manufacture will have been cancelled out when the grenades have reached the issue stage.

The grenades are anchored in position in the case by means of a long metal pin which can be withdrawn the required distance to enable the grenades to be removed one at a time.

Detonator assemblies are issued by the manufacturers packed separately in cardboard tubes, each of which contains

PLATE 5

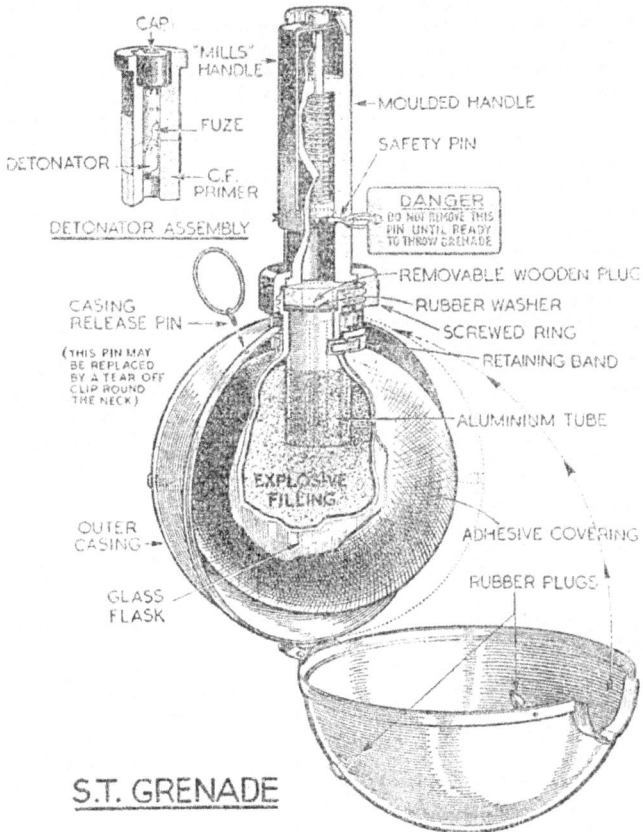

DETONATOR ASSEMBLY

CAP

"MILLS" HANDLE

FUZE

DETONATOR

C.F. PRIMER

MOULDED HANDLE

SAFETY PIN

DANGER
DO NOT REMOVE THIS PIN UNTIL READY TO THROW GRENADE

CASING RELEASE PIN

(THIS PIN MAY BE REPLACED BY A TEAR OFF CLIP ROUND THE NECK)

REMOVABLE WOODEN PLUG

RUBBER WASHER

SCREWED RING

RETAINING BAND

ALUMINIUM TUBE

EXPLOSIVE FILLING

OUTER CASING

GLASS FLASK

ADHESIVE COVERING

RUBBER PLUGS

S.T. GRENADE

five units. These cardboard tubes carrying the detonator assemblies are then packed in boxes of 100.

Clips are provided inside the lid of the metal case carrying the grenades and, if desired, the cardboard tubes can be clipped in position in the lids so that the detonator assemblies are included in the grenade carrying case.

Preparing the grenade for use. Do not remove the metal outer casing. First unscrew the moulded ring which will allow the handle to come away.

Inside the neck of the flask will be found a wooden disc. Remove this and discard it. An aluminium tube will be revealed. On no account must this be disturbed. Obtain a detonator assembly and drop it into place in the aluminium tube. Then replace the handle and screw the ring down tightly. The grenade is now primed.

Handle mechanism. Handles are sent out properly cocked and need not be dismantled or tested.

The striker mechanism in the handle is of a very simple type. Behind the striker head, which can be seen inside the handle when it is removed, is a powerful spring tending to force it down. This movement is prevented by a round nut on the striker spindle engaging a fork on the " Mills " handle. Any appreciable movement of the striker head is also prevented by the safety pin when it is in position.

If the safety pin is removed, movement of the striker is still prevented so long as the " Mills " handle is gripped against the side of the moulded handle. When the grip is released, so that the " Mills " handle is not retained, it will fly off and allow the striker to descend.

The striker is not released until the " Mills " handle has opened out to an angle of about 60 degrees from the moulded handle.

If the firing mechanism is tested it can be recocked by forcing up the striker head against its spring, slipping the " Mills " handle back into place and inserting the safety pin.

Before replacing the cocked handle in a live grenade, see that the safety pin is securely home and that the ends are apart about $\frac{1}{8}$ inch. There is then no chance of the pin slipping out by accident.

Throwing the live grenade. On taking up position, remove the adhesive tape, if any, round the outer casing. Pulling out the pin and releasing the clip holding the outer casing will then cause it to drop off. Let the grenade hang down when releasing the casing so that the two halves drop clear without coming into contact with the adhesive.

Be careful not to allow the exposed grenade to touch anything or it will stick to it. If the surface is not damaged the case can be replaced with care should the opportunity for throwing pass.

Hold the throwing handle in such a way that the metal " Mills " handle is gripped securely against the main portion. Now remove the labelled safety pin. The grenade is still safe so long as the " Mills " handle is not released. On throwing the grenade the " Mills " handle will spring off. Five seconds later detonation will occur. Before this happens the operator must take cover, as although the effect of the explosive is localized, pieces of the handle may be thrown back.

Tactical use of the S.T. grenade. The S.T. grenade is most effective against baby tanks and armoured cars having plating under 1 inch in thickness. It is not effective against plating exceeding this thickness.

Medium or heavy tanks encountered will probably be vulnerable only on the roofs, engine casing and under parts.

The S.T. grenade should be considered as a portable demolition charge which can be quickly and easily applied. One of the safest and easiest methods of application is to drop the grenade from the upstairs window of a building overlooking a road along which a tank is proceeding.

Alternatively, these grenades may be used from some form of ambush within ten or fifteen yards from a road or track along which tanks are likely to pass. A position on a bank overlooking such a road has obvious advantages.

The use of a smoke screen for such operations should be considered. Some form of road block may also prove most useful.

For use during a night raid on tank parks the S.T. grenade is an ideal weapon. It can be planted by hand instead of thrown so long as the operator retreats in such a direction that he is protected from the explosion by part of the tank.

If desired, the grenade can be planted in position and fired by pulling out the safety pin with a long piece of string. When this method is adopted it is essential first to close the ends of the safety pin to make sure that it will slip out easily.

When applying an S.T. grenade by hand, it must be banged down with considerable force to ensure that the flask breaks and that as large an area of contact as possible is obtained. The bigger the area of contact, the more effective will be the explosion.

Throwing practice and instructions. Practice is essential in the throwing of S.T. grenades if good results are to be obtained

—especially against moving targets. Dummy grenades made of wood but proportioned and weighted to correspond exactly with live grenades are issued for this purpose. If they are thrown to fall against a soft target they will last some time.

After a fair amount of practice the average man should be able to throw S.T. grenades a maximum distance of 20 yards and hit a target with fair accuracy 15 yards away on level ground. Throwing from a slit trench will perhaps reduce the distance to 10 yards.

In the open the grenade may be thrown overarm or by lobbing. From a slit trench it can only be thrown overarm.

For instruction purposes a supply of unfilled grenades is available. These grenades are issued in the same cases as the filled ones, but the case marking states that they are unfilled. They are, of course, about 1½ lb. lighter than filled grenades and are not intended for throwing practice.

THE HAND PERCUSSION GRENADE

(To be issued later)

PLATE 6

THE HAND PERCUSSION GRENADE

(To be issued later)

THE HARVEY FLAME THROWER

1. *The equipment*

The flame thrower, which is mounted on 18-inch wheels and can be transported very much in the manner of a porter's barrow, consists of the following parts :—

 i. *A vertical cylinder* of 22 gallons capacity, fitted with a filling hole, safety valve, connections for pressure bottle and recording instruments and hose connector.
 ii. *Pressure bottle.* A standard nitrogen bottle of 40 cubic feet capacity.
 iii. *Hose.* 25 feet of 2-inch armoured flexible hose connected to the base of the cylinder and terminating in a 4-foot metal pipe carrying the nozzle.
 iv. *Nozzle.* A ¾-inch commercial nozzle attached to the pipe.
 v. *Igniting rod* to carry the cotton waste and paraffin for ignition.
 vi. *Support* or stake on which the pipe carrying the nozzle can be traversed or elevated.

2. *Method of operation*

The method of operation of the equipment is as follows :—

 i. The support is driven about 2 feet into the ground.
 ii. The hose is uncoiled, the nozzle supported on its stand, and the igniting rod fixed in position.
 iii. The filling hole plug is removed and the apparatus filled with creosote, leaving approximately 10 per cent. of air space in the container and the plug is replaced.
 iv. The nozzle is unscrewed, a standard ¾-inch cork is inserted *from the inside* and pressed in *finger tight.* The nozzle is then replaced *hand tight* on its washer.
 v. The igniting rod is provided with a pad of cotton waste which is soaked with paraffin, the pad being about 2 feet in front of the nozzle.
 vi. The nozzle operator takes up his position in rear of the stand to direct the nozzle.
 vii. The second operator lights the cotton waste, returns to the cylinder and opens the nitrogen bottle to full capacity as rapidly as possible.
 viii. When the pressure is sufficient, the cork is ejected from the nozzle and the following jet of creosote is ignited as it passes over the flaming cotton waste. The duration of the flame is 10 seconds.

36

PLATE 7

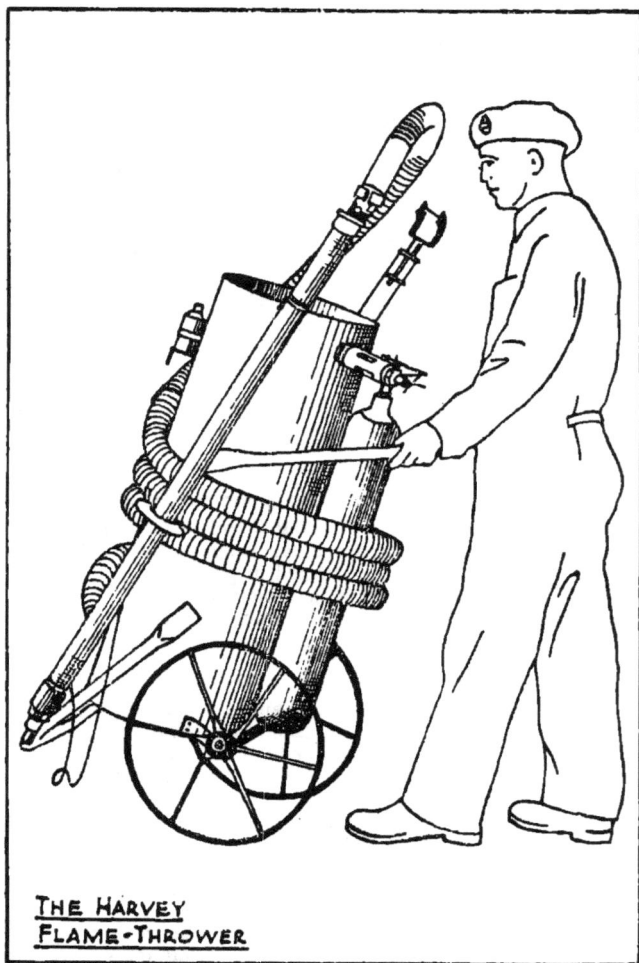

THE HARVEY
FLAME-THROWER

PLATE 8

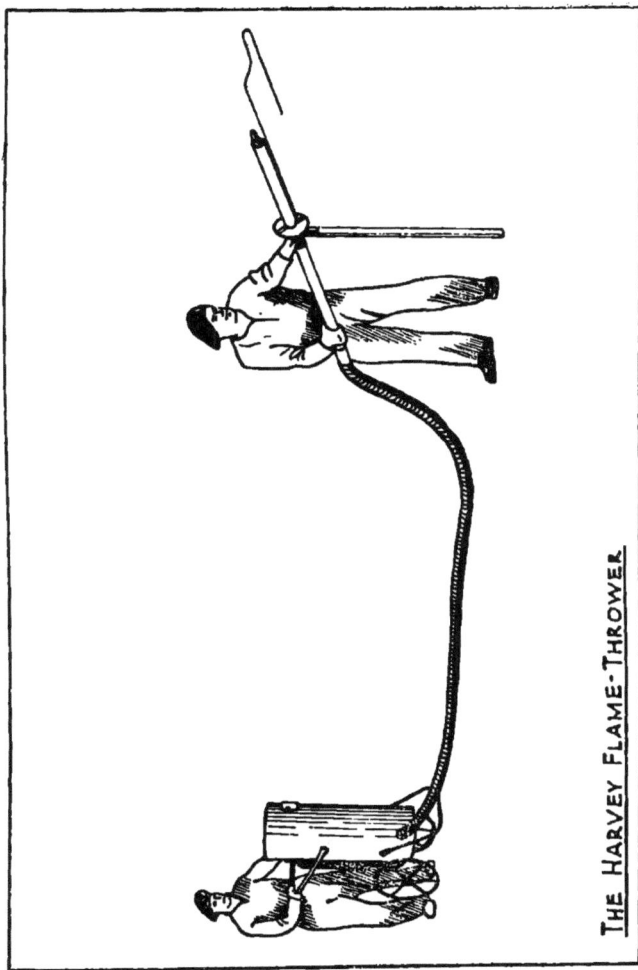

THE HARVEY FLAME-THROWER

THE NORTHOVER (BOTTLE) MORTAR

(To be issued later)

PLATE 9

THE NORTHOVER (BOTTLE) MORTAR

(To be issued later)

APPENDICES

PLATES

DISTRIBUTION

TRAINING MANUALS, TEXT BOOKS AND INSTRUCTIONS

The backbone of all successful armies is its training and tactics. The Naval and Military Press publishes many such manuals of instruction – all perviously long out of print . So, whether your interest lies in the infantry and cavalry tactics of the earliest regiments of the British army in the 18th century, or the weapons manuals and firing instructions of 20th century warfare, the Naval and Military Press has the right book for you.

www.naval-military-press.com

MINES AND BOOBY TRAPS 1943

This is a War Office pamphlet, issued mid-war, in 1943. Its purpose is to introduce sappers to mines commonly used by the British Army – and how to deal with similar devices set by the Germans. The devices described and illustrated cover British anti-tank; grenade; shrapnel and assorted booby trap switches. Enemy mines are covered in chapter 2 with anti-tank, Teller mine types; French anti-tank; Hungarian; anti-personnel German and Italian; and igniters.This is a concise but comprehensive guide for British Army sappers in the art of demining or mine clearance.

9781474539395

THE .303 LEWIS GUN

Illustrated with good clear line drawings this 1941 weapon guide tells the Home Guard Volunteer how to use the 303 Lewis Gun effectively against the invading enemy.A reprint of an original handbook for the .303 Lewis Gun, that was first published in 1941. This book is a practical guide to the handling and maintenance of this iconic weapon.In the crisis following the Fall of France, where a large part of the British Army's equipment had been lost up to and at Dunkirk, stocks of Lewis guns in both .303 and .30-06 were hurriedly pressed back into service, primarily for Home Guard use. Full of fascinating information, this book taught the user the guns capabilities and all he needed to know about maintenance and combat use. Number 2 in the wartime Nicholson & Watson "Know Your Weapons" series, that offer all the important information in a more vivid style than an official publication. Illustrated with good clear line drawings.

9781474539456

ANTI-TANK WEAPONS
Smash The Tank

An insight into the amateur side of World War 2. Diagrams illustrate the main points and the devices, such as the Thermos Bomb;Phosrhorus Bomb;Sticky Bombs; that could be cobbled together from household items are described.This pamphlet was available to the Home Guard and describes the German tank and how to destroy it. It is an early War publication c1940, dealing with the light tanks used by the Germans, also the author gives examples of anti-tank actions in the Spanish Civil War, in which he took part. I'ts is a fascinating look at the "enthusiastic" approach to killing tanks.
9781474539449

TANK HUNTING AND DESTRUCTION 1940

The stated object for the distributing of this War Office manual was as "A guide and help to troops who have the determination and nerve to destroy tanks at close quarters". Intended for fighting on home soil after the very real possibility of a full German invasion, "Operation Sea Lion", this is a remarkable if somewhat naive snap shot of Britain state of preparedness,in her most dangerous hour.
The contents details Tank hunting, Tank characteristics,Tactical action,Road blocks,ambushes Ect,also includes an interesting appendix on Molotov Cocktails, and materials on other ways to destroy tanks.
9781474539401

TROOP TRAINING FOR LIGHT TANK TROOPS NOVEMBER 1939

Very early War tactics pertaining to various aspects of training with and employing armour in the British Army. Covering in concise detail that which a Light tank crew needed to know to be effective in action.
In the early years of the war, Germany held the initiative. German forces used Blitzkrieg tactics in France in 1940, making full use of the speed and armour of tanks to break through enemy defences. It was clear that German tank tactics had evolved during the inter-war period. By contrast, Britain and the Allies were playing catch-up.
9781474539302

JAPANESE WEAPONS ILLUSTRATED
September 1944

This period 'Restricted' laced binding manual was intended to be an aid to the identification of Japanese Army equipment, with sections covering: Tanks, both two-man, Tankette, light and medium; Armoured Cars; Self-Propelled Guns; Anti-Tank Guns; Artillery; Anti-Aircraft Guns; Mortars & Grenade Dischargers; Small Arms; Flamethrowers etc. Produced one year before the surrender of Japan, this work gives a good overview of the weapons the allies would find, fighting an army that despite being on the back foot, was still capable of stiff resistance in an almost entirely defensive role..
9781474539432

NOTES ON THE GERMAN ARMY-WAR
December 1940

An early war 393-page 'Notes' periodical manual from December 1940. It is a detailed review, for use in the field. The manual looks at every aspect of the "Blitzkrieg" German Army (and, to some extent, the Air Force) and gives details as known at the time.

It covers the fighting arms and the services behind them – tactics, organisation, weapons and equipment. It usefully also includes a colour section on uniforms and insignia, a black-and-white plate section of small arms, infantry support and anti-tank weapons, artillery and AFVs. A series of pull-outs related to the text covering tanks etc. are also reproduced.

This is an important first-class picture of the complex fighting machine that was the German Army at the end of the campaigns of 1940, only six months before the invasion of Russia.
9781474539203

GERMAN MINES AND TRAPS

Mid-1940 War Office manual with details of German mines, both the Teller and S-mine (Bouncing Betty) are covered, with techniques for disarming. Good clear full-page line drawings give both practical and technical information. Highly recommended because of the illustrations, which show how these devices worked and the components.
9781474535809

NOTES ON ENEMY ARMY IDENTIFICATIONS ITALY
October 1941

This period handbook was published to give British military personnel a better understanding of the principal characteristics of both the Italian army and the Black Shirt Militia under active service conditions , it is dated October 1941.

It begins with a description of distinctive branches, or specialities, the most characteristic of which was the arm of the Royal Carabinieri, a semi-military body occupying, historically, the senior position in the Army. Other specialities included the Grenadiers of Sardinia, the Bersaglieri, the Alpini and the San Marco Marine Regiment

The handbook then goes on to show, in order, the organisation of Command and Staff, of formations (corps and divisions) and of the arms and services; services, supply and transportation; ranks, plates (many in colour) cover uniforms, insignia, medals and decorations; armament and equipment and a chapter on the Air Force, There are chapters on tactical doctrine and principles of employment, on permanent fortifications, camouflage and abbreviations. Finally there is a brief index.

9781474539746

MANUAL OF GUERILLA TACTICS
Specially Prepared And Based On Lessons From
The Spanish And Russian Campaigns

One of the excellent, concise Bernards Pocket Books, intended to show members of the Home Guard and the regular forces that war is not conducted in a gentlemanly way – it is kill or be killed.

9781474539463

THE OFFENSIVE OF SMALL UNITS
September 1916

This is a periodical tactical manual from 1916, it focuses on the manner in which the French organised and executed their attacks and counterattacks . Summarised from the French, it lays out the process by which to operate in attacks on the German trenches. Focused purely on the operation of infantry, the purpose of this British translation is to give small infantry units the benefit of the French experience in regard to the best methods of combat, in offensive operations.

9781474537971

TRENCH WARFARE
Notes on attack and defence, February 1915

This important period manual was published in early 1915 when hope of a quick ending to the war disappeared, and trench warfare had begun to dominate the Western Front.

The manual strives to instil an offensive spirit and gives practical examples on: Close quarter, local, methods of successful warfare, and German attacks. The salient points to gather were preparation and co-operation between artillery and infantry, and that the capture of trenches is easier than their retention. Two plates illustrating tactics complete this official publication.

9781474539807

Ministry Of Home Security
OBJECTS DROPPED FROM THE AIR 1941

An illustrated Official and confidential publication, covering the many and varied types of objects that were falling from principally German aircraft during the Second phase of the blitz, including high explosives,incendiary bombs and small arms ammunition. Complete with 8 page addendum.

9781783319541

THE MUSKETRY INSTRUCTIONS
FOR THE GERMAN INFANTRY 1887
(Schiessvorshrift fur die Infanterie)
Translated for the intelligence Division War Office

Translated for the War Office by Colonel C W Bowdler Bell

A facsimile that includes the supplement for the German Infantry for 1887. Musketry exercises were intended to give the infantry instruction in shooting, to make effective use of their firearm in battle. As such the manual shows important details designed to make the infantry soldier battle-ready by the end of his first year of service. Instruction is subdivided into Preparatory exercises; Target practice; Field firing; Instructional firing; Inspection in musketry; Proving the rifle M/61.84 and revolver M/83. Many black powder weapons were still used, mainly for training purposes, up to end of the First World War.

9781783313631

www.ingramcontent.com/pod-product-compliance
Lightning Source LLC
Chambersburg PA
CBHW071645040426
42452CB00009B/1770